GOOD GIRL TRAUMA IS NOT MY DRAMA!

Healing Fawn(ing) Trauma and Rediscovering Authenticity

Table of Contents

Letter to Reader

Preface

Chapter 1: Understanding Fawn Trauma

Chapter 2: Unraveling the Roots of Fawn Trauma

Chapter 3: Removing the Masks We Wear

Chapter 4: Cultivating Self-Compassion

Chapter 5: Setting Healthy Boundaries

Chapter 6: Embracing Authenticity

Chapter 7: Nurturing Authentic Relationships

Chapter 8: Self-Care for Authentic Living

Chapter 9: Building Resilience

Embracing Your Authentic Self

Appendix: Additional Resources

- Books, Articles, and Websites
- Support Groups and Therapeutic Services

Note: It is important to note that while I have poured my heart into researching and writing about fawn trauma, I am not a medical professional and this guide does not constitute medical advice. Instead, it provides a comprehensive understanding of fawn trauma, explores its origins, and offers practical strategies for overcoming its impact based on research and my own lived experience. It emphasizes self-compassion, boundary-setting, authenticity, and healing techniques to guide individuals toward reclaiming their true selves and living a life free from the constraints of fawn trauma. Through introspection, self-reflection exercises, and therapeutic approaches, readers can embark on a transformative journey toward healing, growth, and resilience. Remember, healing is a unique and ongoing process, and this book is intended to be a supportive resource for that journey.

Letter to You

(Good Girl, Good Guy, Fawn Trauma Crusher)!

Hello Friend,

I want you to know that you are not defined by your past experiences, and you have the strength within you to overcome the challenges you face because of fawn trauma. Your path of healing and growth is on-going, and I believe in your ability to rediscover your strength and to redefine your sense of self.

You will feel overwhelmed at times because healing is a process. You make progress every day, even if it doesn't always feel that way. Each step you take toward acknowledging your feelings and working through them is a step toward liberation from the grip of trauma.

At the end of each chapter you will find questions to help you rewrite your narrative. Confronting your trauma is a testament to your courage and resilience. This journey may have its challenges, so celebrate each victory, no matter how big or small, along the way.

You'll find valuable insights, practical steps, and strategies to make a difference in your healing journey. Taking action is incredibly helpful for individuals recovering from fawn trauma response because it helps us embrace our authenticity.

The emphasis on self-compassion, seeking professional support, setting boundaries, and cultivating self-awareness is particularly powerful. These aspects are essential in creating a solid foundation for healing and growth. Each chapter's interactive format, plus the encouragement to reflect on your thoughts and experiences, adds a personalized touch that can make your recovery process more effective and relatable.

I've approached this topic with care and empathy using my own experiences as the foundation. I know you will find this a thoughtful and supportive guide for your own journey.

You are not alone. Lean on the support of those who care about you – friends, family, therapists, or support groups – for comfort, guidance, and understanding. It's okay to ask for help when you need it.

You have the power to transform your trauma into strength. Your past does not have to dictate your future. Every step you take toward healing is a step toward regaining control over your life and embracing your authentic self.

Believe in your own resilience, in your ability to overcome, and in your worthiness of a life filled with joy, love, and fulfillment. You are capable of breaking free from the chains of fawn trauma and emerging as a more empowered and self-assured individual.

Your journey may have started with pain, but it can lead to a future of hope and healing. Keep moving forward, keep believing in yourself, and keep your eyes on the brighter days that lie ahead.

With unwavering support,

Tracey

Preface

A best friend is always there for you, right? I will give my last. Call me anytime of the day or night and I will be there. People call me amazing. They call me loyal. I am always supportive and dependable. I speak highly of my friends to others and will make the best out of every negative situation concerning them. I consult with them and provide a positive outlook about their problems. I am their number one fan.

Tina called me to tell me about her new car. She was so excited! She bought a brand-new Ford Focus with all the bells and whistles. She traded in her old car and put down $2,500. Her monthly payments were set at a whopping $725 per month. Tina did not see anything wrong with it until the excitement wore off when she counted her money and realized she overextended herself.

She turned to me for help, and I dove into her situation to save the day, putting everything else aside. I learned Tina had three days to change her mind, so I went into action on her behalf to get both her money and her trade-in back.

Next, I took her to the credit union to get prequalified for a car loan and to connect her with a car dealership where she landed a better deal; less expensive car, no money down, and a great allowance for her trade-in. Tina's car note fit in her budget, and she was so excited, she opened a savings account at the credit union with the $2,500 she used as her downpayment for her original deal.

Sabrina called me because she was nervous about giving a big presentation at work. She needed to create the presentation slides but had no clue how to start. I asked for her topic and information she would cover and got to work creating the presentation for Sabrina. I added talking notes and even practiced with her so that the presentation would be a success. It was perfect! Sabrina received high accolades from the attendees and was recognized for a job well done by her leadership team! The thing is, of course, Sabrina did not ask me to take on the task of completing the presentation. Sabrina only wanted suggestions and to be pointed in the right direction.

Channing needed someone to talk to. He was going through a divorce, needed a place to stay, wanted to find a better job, and wanted to start life over in a new state. He called me for help, advice, and to be a listening ear. I was there for Channing throughout the entire ordeal. He stayed with me until he found his own place. When he settled in at my home, I researched jobs for him and even completed online applications for him. He acquired a new job paying twice as much as his previous position, including relocation costs and a signing bonus. Once again, my friend never asked me to do anything other than listen to him.

I always find a way to help others, sometimes to my detriment, but who is there for me? I can't point to this person or to that friend because I am not comfortable telling people what I need or when I need it. Staying closed-off from others, including those I would describe as part of my closest circle, caused health issues because of my acute feelings of loneliness, abandonment, and rejection. Still, I ignored my own needs and desires and sabotaged my own happiness in a variety of ways. I found it extremely hard to share my needs with others and tried to find solutions to my problems on my own. I retreated into isolation when I needed help the most.

Then, I found love with someone who melted my heart. He knew how to satisfy my needs and intuitively how to take care of my wants. I never had to ask for anything. He paid close attention during intimate conversations. He celebrated me when I accomplished a goal, and he held me in his arms when I needed covering. He made me feel safe and desired, and he showed me how to be loved.

But, I was so uncomfortable receiving the same support and love I gave others that I sabotaged our relationship by ignoring him on a basic level and by refusing to go deeper with him. I loved him on the surface, and he even told me how I made every encounter feel like we were on vacation. Whether we went out to dinner or I cooked at home, the moment was special.

On the other hand, he felt like I was not interested or I had interests in someone else because while we were together, it was magical, but when we weren't together, he felt forgotten. He witnessed how I cared for my family and friends, how I gave my time to causes, and found a way to support my community but never gave that same energy to him. I blocked love, especially his love. It was so easy to give it to those who didn't reciprocate, but extremely difficult to give love to a man who only wanted to love me.

Losing the love that felt so perfect caused me to evaluate my actions and fueled my desire to find out why I didn't know how to accept the love and support I so willingly gave. I listened to podcasts and watched videos. I started following creators on TikTok talking about mental health and discovered I was not alone. The key word? Trauma.

I researched the types of traumas and learned about the trauma affecting me most: fawn trauma. When I heard someone call it, "Good Girl Trauma," I definitely related!

Deep down, we all crave connection, acceptance, and a sense of belonging. We want to be understood and acknowledged. For some of us, this longing comes with a fear of being pushed away or left behind. Past hurts, shaped by our childhoods and what society expects of us, can push us to hide our true feelings and needs. This often leads us to a survival tactic called the fawn response.

Fawn is one of the four trauma responses; fight, flight, and freeze are the other three. Each describes a manner in which we react to tough times. The fawn response is marked by always trying to please others, even if it means ignoring what we truly need. We try to win people over when fighting back, running away, or freezing up seem pointless or unsafe. The fawn response is both a last-ditch effort and an avoidance technique to find safety and closeness, a way to cope with the hurt and vulnerability we feel deep inside.

We're going on a journey of discovery and healing, to dive into the world of fawn trauma and dig into where it comes from, how it shows up in our lives, and what it does to every facet of our lives. Together, we'll untangle the habits that made us put aside who we really are to fit in and gain approval from others.

Think about what comes next as a map to help you overcome your fawn trauma. We're going to explore ways to heal, do some soul-searching, and pick up useful tricks along the way. Through this, we'll learn how to be kinder to ourselves, set better limits, embrace our true selves, and gain the strength to deal with life's tougher moments.

But here's the deal: this book isn't a quick fix. I didn't write this to serve as some magic trick that makes everything better. Healing from fawn trauma is a personal journey, and it's different for everyone. You need time, patience, and to stick with it. Inside these pages, you'll find ideas, tools, and things to do that will help you feel whole again.

Remember, you're not on your own here. Plenty of others have been through—or are still going through—something similar to what you are. As we dig into this together, remember that healing isn't a straight line, and it doesn't have a deadline. Healing is continuous, and you take it one step at a time. Every step counts, no matter how small.

So, my friend, let's take this big journey together. Let's shine a light into the shadows of fawn trauma, ditch the masks we've been wearing, and come out as our real selves. It won't always be easy, but you will be empowered and free. This journey will be worth it. Let's get started!

Chapter 1:
Understanding Fawn Trauma

When things get tough, our brains kick into action to keep us safe by initiating one of four responses: fight, flight, freeze, and fawn. While most folks have heard of fight and flight, freeze and fawn often fly under the radar.

The fawn response, the star of our show, is a survival strategy hardwired within us. When we feel threatened or in a dangerous situation, we lean toward fawning because we have a history of people-pleasing to stay safe through the worst part of the cycle of abuse.

I lived through this cycle of abuse for far too long. I worked for an organization that had a mission of educating and promoting financial empowerment for all. I always shared the vision of empowering others to be the best version of themselves, especially regarding wealth creation.

I started the job at this organization with enthusiasm. My manager, LaTrice, was initially very supportive and charming as a boss, but, over time, her true nature was revealed.

I noticed that Latrice was becoming increasingly critical and demanding. She frequently changed her mind about project details, leaving me frustrated and anxious about meeting deadlines. She started to berate me in meetings and belittled me in front of my colleagues. Latrice gave me tasks with unrealistic expectations and frequently blamed me for the team's failures, even when the situations were beyond my control.

After each episode of abuse, Latrice attempted to make amends by praising me or offering empty apologies. She promised to treat me better and give me recognition for my hard work and continuously manipulated me into staying.

When things were calm, I experienced moments of relief because she seemed supportive and friendly again. However, it was short-lived, and the tension would begin building, and the cycle would start again.

I feared losing my job and wanted to keep the peace, so I started people-pleasing. I worked long hours, took on excessive responsibilities, and constantly sought her approval, even to the detriment of my own well-being.

This is classic fawn trauma behavior in the workplace, which often mirrors our experiences at home. We automatically put others first, push down our own wants, and go out of our way to make others happy, all to create a false sense of safety and connection.

Understanding the Fawn Response and Its Impact

I remember the day my mother and father separated like it was yesterday. I was Daddy's little girl. We had a special bond and I thought he was the best dad in the world! He was perfect in my eyes. But, on that day, he asked me to choose to live with him or my mother and gave me all of the reasons why life would be better with him. I was only six years old and my mother was sick. She suffered from Cushing's Disease, hypothyroidism, Type 1 diabetes, rheumatoid arthritis, high blood pressure, and had been resuscitated only moments from death twice before I turned six. I couldn't leave her alone to care for herself and my two brothers, with the youngest being only three years old. My older brother was twelve, but I was a little mama. I had to make sure everyone was okay, especially my mom.

I thought Daddy would definitely understand. Afterall, he was my dad, the best dad in the world, and he had to understand that I could never leave my mom.

She was the sweetest, most caring person I ever knew. Everyone loved her because she sincerely loved them back from a place in her heart that I have never known or felt from anyone else. She was a prayer warrior, an educator, a fighter, and a friend. She was beautiful, smart, comedic, and she loved to draw and write poetry and short stories.

My mom always reassured me that I could and would be whatever I wanted to be. She was the most amazing person, and she left a lasting impression on everyone who knew her, even my dad! He always spoke highly of her, even after their separation, and how she had so much compassion for others especially in light of the health issues she had to endure.

She died when she was just 49 after suffering a heart attack. She gave me the best 26 years of my life and I will forever be grateful for how she raised me by instilling in me faith, hope, and love. I could have never left her.

My dad looked at me like I had just shoved a knife in his heart. At just six years old, I felt like I broke his heart. I also worried that if I left my mom, she would have died from a broken heart. It was a hard position to be in because my mother also told me it was my choice. She just wanted me to be happy. If I had gone with my dad, he promised I would have had anything I wanted. It would have been me and him against the world! I would have had all of the material things I could have dreamed of. My youngest brother was so little and attached to my mom that I don't recall my dad asking him to come along. My older brother's dad was my mom's first husband and had passed away.

But, I needed nurturing, support, and guidance. I didn't believe nor do I believe now that I would have received those things from him. He worked all of the time and even though we had a wonderful relationship, he never had to handle the day-to-day necessities of getting me to school, assisting with homework, or combing my hair, but he could definitely cook. He actually taught my mom how to cook. He owned a community grocery store and a cab company and served as vice president of the local union for cab drivers. However, my dad never accepted my oldest brother as his own, and he made a distinct difference between us. It was so pronounced that I began to mirror my dad's attitude and behavior toward my older brother until I was two. At two, I was playing with a door stopper and threw it at my older brother, barely missing his head. The terror in his eyes shook me to my core. I cried and trembled so intensely that my mother had to console both of us. It was like a lightbulb went off and I realized that I could have hurt him. I held on to his arm and laid my head on his shoulder all night long sobbing for what I did.

Despite being so young, I believe I realized the impact of my actions at that very moment and began to see my dad's actions in a different light. I started to mimic the actions of my mother and became more loving and kind, and inclusive and considerate towards my brothers and my mom. I became "little mama"!

As a girl, I needed more structure, and I needed my mom for all the reasons I've listed and so many more. There was an additional reason to stay with my mom; Daddy had a girlfriend who disliked everything about me and his relationship with me. She referred to me as his daughter and called my brothers her stepsons. She was nothing like my mother and other stepmothers who raised their kids to know and love each other. She only had time for my brothers and made it very clear that she wanted nothing to do with the girls.

Our family tree has even more branches because my dad was married twice before my mom, giving me four older sisters and a brother. If that wasn't complicated enough, after Daddy and Mom divorced, he married his girlfriend and fathered two daughters with the babysitter while being married to her. His home was definitely not an environment conducive for raising a daughter, and I know I made the right choice.

Still, I never stopped feeling guilty for not going with my dad and tried to make it up to him. I called him every day and promised to spend weekends with him, but that wasn't good enough. Wow, writing these memories made me realize how traumatic my youth was. I tried to be the most polite, obedient child I could be for my dad. I made good grades so that he would be proud of me. I helped my mom with my brothers and made sure she was okay while trying not to bother my dad by asking him to help out when we needed him. Nothing I did rekindled the relationship we had before he left. I knew he loved me, but I felt like I broke the bond we had, so I tried daily to find ways to mend it.

I know I made the right decision, but he clearly didn't agree. Instead, he made promises he never kept. Honestly, I felt I deserved it since I disappointed him so badly. He always promised to come to my recitals, plays, graduations, awards ceremonies, birthday parties, and any other events that were near and dear to my heart. He missed them all, and I always forgave him. I would sit at the window every day hoping he would come by as he said he would. If he happened to stop by, it was simply a drive by. He would blow the horn and we would go out to the car. Dad would say hello, smile, and tell us he would see us later.

When I graduated from high school with honors and several scholarships, I was so proud. My mother was in the hospital in the ICU and not expected to live. I begged my dad to come to my graduation, and he promised to be there. I stood on the graduation stage at the Atlanta Civic Center and scanned the audience for a glimpse of him. You couldn't miss him. He was 6'3" and 275 pounds, brown skinned, broad shoulders, a medium length afro, and greenish-gray eyes with a swag that made women, young and old, swoon over him. My aunt saved a seat for him near the front, but it remained empty for the entire ceremony. He was a no-call-no-show.

I was devastated and I took it upon myself to do something to be a better daughter and a better person. Never mind that he was the adult and should have been a better father and a better person, but that's the adult-me talking. At the time, I felt like I had to make up for not being there for him when he needed me the most. I simply wanted my dad to love me.

After the graduation ceremony, I went directly to the hospital to show my diploma and accolades to my mom. She was so proud of me and promised me a celebration when she was better. When she recovered enough to come home, she baked me a cake and we had the best time. My dad never gave an explanation for his absence nor did he congratulate me on a job well done. We never spoke of it again. It was never reconciled. I just swallowed the pain of disappointment and accepted the time and attention he gave me while making excuses for the times he didn't show up.

My fawning response comes in large part from the inability to overcome the consequences I lived as a child who was asked to make an adult decision that wasn't my responsibility. I realize now that I used fawning as a way to avoid hurt and rejection. I gave up my own boundaries and real feelings for acceptance, validation, and inclusion from my father that never actually materialized.

The impact of fawn trauma can be a real bummer. Always focusing on what others need wears down your self-esteem, twists your sense of self, and makes a mess of genuine relationships. Fawn trauma leaves you feeling empty, mad, and disconnected from your own wants and needs.

The first step to healing fawn trauma is recognizing what it is. Fawning shows up as being way too agreeable, putting others before yourself, and freaking out about even the possibility of being rejected. Take a good look at how you act and how you relate to others to begin understanding why you struggle and what old wounds you carry around.

Do any of the following sound familiar?

- You always try to make others happy, even if it inconveniences or hurts you.
- You feel super anxious about potentially being left out or dumped by others.
- You find it tough to refuse others or to set personal boundaries, which often means you get taken advantage of.
- You seek approval from others to feel good about yourself.
- You keep your feelings locked up to keep the peace and avoid fights.

- You have relationships where your happiness is based on making others happy.

Knowing these signs helps us untangle the knots of fawn trauma and how it complicates our lives. Once we're aware, we can heal and learn who we really are. In the chapters ahead, we'll dig even deeper into why fawn trauma begins, how we put up walls to protect ourselves, and we'll set off on a big journey toward healing and finding our true selves. Just remember, you're not alone in this. Let's tackle the twists and turns of fawn trauma and find our way to feeling whole and real.

Reflections

> Now that you're familiar with the concept of fawn trauma response, write down at least two examples of how it shows up in your life as an adult.
>
> _____
> _____
> _____
> _____

What are you feeling right now?

Chapter 2:
Unraveling the Roots of Fawn Trauma

To uncover how fawn trauma happens, we need to rewind to when we were kids. Those early years shaped how we see the world, ourselves, and other people. So many of us learned how to deal with tough stuff. When we grow up with neglect, abuse, inconsistent care, and without trusted connections, fawn trauma begins. As children, we learned what we needed, wanted, and felt didn't really matter. Our feelings were ignored, or maybe we were punished for expressing ourselves. To stay safe, we started fawning – doing whatever it took to avoid trouble and stay on the right side of the adult(s) with the power.

We got really good at picking up on other people's feelings and needs, which meant ignoring our own. This survival trick stuck around as we grew up and affected how we related to others.

As my story illustrates, childhood is where fawn trauma most often starts, and it just keeps going from there. We choose partners who shine under our care then wilt with disappointment when we aren't as attentive, prompting us to refocus on them and not ourselves. We want our children to never question our love, so we put them at the center of everything we do, erasing our separate sense of self.

We also have generations of messaging in the media, scripted television, and now social media about finding meaning in pleasing others while hiding our real selves. After living the results of fawn behavior — calmer parents, happier boyfriends or girlfriends, thriving children, smiling bosses — we reflexively surround ourselves with people who help us keep the fawning going strong, and most of the time, they aren't aware of it.

We learned through experience that if we want to fit in and do well, we've got to put others first, dodge conflicts, and get a thumbs-up from everyone. Because these messages were constantly reinforced, we locked into fawn trauma, making it a challenge to break free from focusing on making people happy to learn anything real about ourselves.

And if that wasn't enough, things like gender, race, and cultural norms force us into roles or behaviors we often don't think much about until we realize we've been chafing under these definitions. By then, we don't really know how to make the necessary changes, and if we dare to break any of the patterns, we immediately feel the disapproval. Self-preservation takes over, which just keeps the fawn cycle spinning.

Spotting the Behaviors of Fawn Trauma

Seeing fawn trauma for what it is puts us on the path to healing and finding our true selves. Once we see how fawning shows up in our lives, we can start shaking things up.

This is what fawn trauma can look like in our daily lives before we make the daily choice to center our lives around ourselves:

- We give too much, always put others first, and feel bad when we think about ourselves.
- We try hard to please everyone else and often give up what we want or need.
- We bury our feelings, act like a caretaker, and ignore our own needs to keep things smooth.
- We struggle to say no or set boundaries to protect our time and space, afraid of the repercussions if we do.
- We depend on others' approval to feel good about ourselves, which leaves our self-esteem in a constant state of fragility.

Untangling the grip of fawn trauma starts your journey of meeting and getting to know yourself. You deserve to treat yourself kindly, set better boundaries, and break free from the hold of fawning. You have the power to be your true self and build relationships that match who you really are.

Reflections

- What did you learn about the origins of your fawn trauma?

_____
_____
_____
_____
_____
_____
_____
_____
_____
_____
_____
_____
_____
_____

- How do you see it manifest in your behavior?

_____
_____
_____
_____
_____
_____
_____
_____
_____
_____
_____
_____
_____
_____
_____
_____
_____
_____
_____
_____
_____

Consider working with a therapist or counselor who specializes in trauma and can guide you through the recovery process. They can provide valuable insights, tools, and support tailored to your specific needs.

- Name of Therapist/Counselor:

  _____
  _____
  _____

- Date of appointment:

  _____
  _____

- Plan of action with therapist/counselor:

  _____
  _____
  _____
  _____
  _____

Chapter 3:
Removing the Masks We Wear

When fawn trauma takes hold, we create a fake version of ourselves. We become whoever we need to be to make others happy and meet their expectations. Our mask hides our real thoughts and feelings and what we truly want. We value fitting in and feeling safe almost more than anything.

The remedy for fawn trauma is more simple than it sounds: authenticity. Embracing and showing our genuine thoughts, feelings, and needs without worrying about what others will say is the answer, but here's the catch—it takes guts and treating ourselves with kindness.

The Role of Shame and Guilt in Fawning

Shame and guilt fuel fawn trauma. Shame tells us we're not good enough as we are, so we need the mask to project the image we think everyone wants from us. We've been taught that putting ourselves first is selfish, so when we do, the guilt is almost unbearable.

We constantly question if saying no to someone made them mad and if we should apologize. We worry we've let them down, even for simple requests such as turning down a meeting for coffee because we might have something else going on or, and this is the hardest one, if we just want to sit at home alone.

Shame takes root when we behaved as our natural selves, and we were put down or disciplined for it. Making a child feel less-than is the quickest and best way to be sure they hide themselves and start fawning to earn positive attention and praise.

Seeing how shame and guilt drive fawning helps us stand up to both and begin to act more kindly toward ourselves. We realize shame and guilt don't own us, and we allow our real selves shine.

Peeling Off the Masks: Self-Reflection

Removing the masks we've worn our entire lives takes courage and intentional, daily practice and self-reflection. It can be painful and exhausting to discover our real selves, but every step is worth it. These exercises can help:

1. **Journaling:** Grab a journal or even just a notebook and a pen. Let your thoughts and feelings flow.

2. **Values Check:** Figure out what you truly believe are the most important qualities in a person and how you can live them. Do you embody these core values today or do you give them up to please others?

3. **Feelings Unveiled:** Start paying attention to your emotions and what they tell you. If you notice you shove them down and do whatever you can to avoid your feelings such as cleaning, exercising, doom scrolling social media, or watching TV, use your journal/notebook to let them out in a safe space.

4. **Boundary Time:** Look at your personal boundaries and be honest about if you

protect your time and space. How often do you let them slide for others? Choose the boundaries most important to you and begin reinforcing them to take back your space and honor your needs. Some examples of protecting personal boundaries include:

1. Work-Life Balance: Set boundaries around your work hours. When you are off, you are off!

2. Personal Space: Define time when you need alone time to recharge.

3. Social Engagements: Be selective about when, where, and with whom you socialize, especially if you need rest.

4. Screen Time: Reduce your screen time on devices especially before bedtime. Schedule time blocks for screen time and stick to it.

5. Family Time: Designate specific family/quality time with loved ones.
6. Self-Care: Make it a priority to exercise and meditate.
7. Saying "No": Learn to say "no" when necessary without compromising your boundaries.
8. Unplugging: Shut off your phone and other devices during meals or at gatherings.
9. Me Time: Time-block solely for yourself to be pampered, to relax or to simply do nothing.
10. Communication: Clearly tell your inner circle (people in your life) about your boundaries.

5. **Love Yourself:** Treat yourself with kindness. Take time to meditate, practice mindfulness and positive self-talk, eat healthier, and

move your body. Invest in your happiness and well-being.

Exercises like these empower us to peel away the layers we've been wearing for too long. Kindness is the greatest gift we can give ourselves as we travel the road to understanding and reclaiming ourselves.

Reflections

- What is the first part of yourself you will no longer hide?

_____
_____
_____
_____
_____
_____
_____
_____
_____
_____

- What values do you hold most dear?

_____
_____
_____
_____
_____
_____
_____
_____
_____
_____
_____
_____
_____
_____
_____
_____

- Cultivate mindfulness and self-reflection to become more aware of your thoughts, emotions, and triggers.

  What does this look like for you?

  _____
  _____

Chapter 4: Cultivating Self-Compassion

Self-compassion is similar to a magical potion for healing fawn trauma. It's all about being as kind, understanding, and accepting of yourself as you would be for a dear friend. When you show yourself compassion, you give yourself permission to be vulnerable, acknowledge your pain, and give yourself the love and care you totally deserve.

Dealing with Your Inner Critic

While you heal, that voice in the back of your mind that tells you not to bother needs to be acknowledged but not given much attention. This big roadblock is your inner critic, and it can get in the way of self-compassion. Fawn trauma often feeds this nagging voice that blames us, makes us feel like we're not enough, and pushes us to make others happy and ourselves a nonfactor in our own lives. This voice is all about making us believe our worth depends on what others think.

Fight back against this inner critic by giving it a name. Hear what it says and think about how someone you love would feel if you said those things to them. They'd be heartbroken, right? So why do we allow this voice to say such awful things to us?

Next, take note of the mean thoughts and counter them with kindness. Creating a phrase you can use whenever your inner critic has something nasty to say can help keep you in a positive frame of mind. This helps you change the story you're telling yourself and creates a more loving inner dialogue.

Practicing Self-Compassion

Self-compassion isn't something you do once in a while. You weave it into your everyday life to help you handle challenges and bumps with grace and strength.

Mindfulness: Try being fully present in every moment. This helps you be kinder to yourself as you observe your thoughts, feelings, and sensations without harsh judgment.

Validation: It's okay to feel whatever arises while you journal, meditate, take a walk, or out of seemingly nowhere. Instead of brushing off your emotions, give them the respect they deserve. Tell yourself that your feelings matter and believe it.

Forgiveness: Let go of blaming yourself for what hasn't gone right. Remember, mistakes are part of being human and a chance to grow and learn.

Loving-Kindness Meditation: Try a meditation where you send yourself good vibes. You can say things like, "May I be happy, may I be safe, may I live with ease." This helps you build self-love and care.

By building self-compassion, you break the chains of the fawn response and step into your true self. As a result, you set better boundaries, listen to and fulfill your needs, and create relationships centered around authenticity and respect.

As we keep moving forward, remember that self-compassion isn't a luxury — it's a must-have and a tool that can turn fawn trauma into strength, wholeness, and living true to yourself. It's how you show deep love to yourself.

Reflections

You understand now why developing a compassionate and non-judgmental attitude toward yourself is so important.

- What phrases will you create to shut down your inner critic?

_____
_____
_____
_____
_____
_____
_____
_____
_____
_____
_____
_____
_____

_____
_____
_____
_____

- Make a list of every good thing about yourself. This can include both material and non-material things. Write them all down.

_____
_____
_____
_____
_____
_____
_____
_____
_____
_____
_____
_____
_____
_____

- Write each letter of your name on a separate line. Find positive words that begin with that letter and write them down.

Chapter 5:
Setting Healthy Boundaries

Boundaries help relationships flourish for all parties involved. When fawn trauma is part of our experience, though, boundaries tend to blur or disappear. We focus on others' needs so much that we forget about our own. Setting good boundaries is the key to taking back your power, building self-respect, and enjoying balanced relationships.

The Lowdown on Boundaries

Boundaries are the rules we set to keep ourselves safe — emotionally and physically. We have the power to decide what's okay and not okay when we interact with others. Healthy boundaries give us the freedom to express our needs, stand up for our values, and create safe spaces in our relationships.

Recognizing Crossed Boundaries

When you suffer from fawn trauma, spotting crossed boundaries can be hard. Some signs of this happening include:

- Feeling uneasy during certain interactions or relationships.
- Always saying yes even when you want to say no.
- Feeling drained, mad, or used.
- Feeling powerless against having your personal space and privacy invaded.
- Ignoring your own needs to make others happy.

It's super important to recognize these signs so you know when it's time to reinforce your weak spots.

Talking About Boundaries and Setting Them

Setting boundaries is like saying, "Hey, this is where I draw the line." Here's how you can do it:

- **Reflect:** Think about what you need, what's important to you, and what makes you comfortable or not.

- **Pinpoint:** Figure out exactly how you need to protect your time, space, and emotions.

- **Talk It Out:** Tell people about your boundaries. Use "I" statements to explain what you need. Be clear and exude confidence.

- **Stick to It:** Keep your boundaries strong. If others keep ignoring them, calmly but firmly remind them. This might mean saying no, setting consequences, or simply removing yourself from situations and the company of those who disrespect your boundaries.

Facing Pushback

Gradually expose yourself to situations where you can practice assertiveness. Start with smaller, low-risk scenarios and gradually work your way up. Celebrate your successes along the way, no matter how small.

When you set boundaries, some folks might not like it and give you a hard time. People used to your fawn response may resist accepting your changes. Stay strong and hold your boundaries. Get support from friends who bolster your efforts, therapists, or groups who can help you stay on track.

Re-assessing Boundaries as You Grow

Remember, your boundaries aren't stuck. As you grow more comfortable with who you are and how you want to live, you can make adjustments. Keep checking with yourself and be true to yourself by making sure your boundaries match what you need.

Reflections

> Look at your closest relationships and write down the boundaries you need to set and/or strengthen for each one.
>
> _____
> _____
> _____

_____
_____
_____
_____
_____
_____
_____
_____
_____

Boundaries often involve telling people, "No." Practice saying, "no" when you would normally say, "yes." How does that feel?

_____
_____
_____
_____
_____
_____
_____
_____
_____

_____
_____
_____
_____
_____
_____
_____

In what way(s) can you be more assertive? Remember to use "I" statements to center your wants and needs.

_____
_____
_____
_____
_____
_____
_____
_____
_____
_____
_____

_____
_____

List situations where you have practiced assertiveness and how you celebrated the experience:

_____
_____
_____
_____
_____
_____
_____
_____
_____
_____
_____
_____
_____
_____
_____
_____

Chapter 6:
Embracing Authenticity

Being authentic means being true to yourself, saying what you mean, feeling what you feel, and wanting what you want – without faking it for anyone. For folks healing from fawn trauma, being true to ourselves — authentic — is a journey, and we must remain thoughtful and kind toward ourselves. Every revelation is another layer peeled away to show the world who you really are.

Off with the Mask

Authenticity requires you to get rid of all the layers that don't serve the real you anyway. Here's how:

- **Know Yourself:** Spend time thinking about what really matters to you. Consider your strengths, your talents, how you enjoy spending time and with whom, and what makes you happy.

- **Spot the Fakes:** Figure out how outside influences, like family or school or society, shaped you. Sort through what's really you from what's been put on you.

- **Bye-Bye Approval:** Let go of needing everyone to like you. You're awesome just being you, and your value isn't tied to what others say.

- **Embrace Being Real:** Let down your walls even when it's tough. Let yourself be seen, and put aside what folks might think. Being real means true connections and a more fulfilling life.

Being Truly You

Being authentic isn't just something you think about – it's just who you are. Here's how to do it:

- **Own Your Truth:** Speak up! Be real about what you think and feel, even if others don't agree. Be honest but respectful, even if it's hard.

- **Create Real Connections:** Build relationships where you don't have to pretend. Hang with people who like you just as you are.

- **Get Creative:** Use art, writing, or whatever you love to show the world who you are.
- **Stay True to Yourself:** Make sure your actions match what you believe in, even when others want you to be different.

Perfectly Imperfect

Being true to yourself isn't about being perfect. It's about loving your uniqueness and being okay with not being flawless. Authentic means being real, especially with your flaws.

The process of overcoming fawn trauma is not easy, so give yourself grace. Your best today may not be the same as your best tomorrow, and that's okay.

Setting Ripples in Motion

When you're real, you create a ripple effect, inspiring others to be real, too. You make deeper connections and better relationships because you attract people into your life who are also authentic. Being who you really are lights up your life.

Reflections

Engage in activities that align with your authentic self rather than simply trying to please others. This will help you develop a stronger sense of identity and personal fulfillment.

> What are some activities that bring you joy, peace, a sense of accomplishment, etc.?

_____
_____
_____
_____
_____
_____
_____
_____
_____
_____
_____

When will you do them?

_____
_____
_____
_____
_____

What external influences will you leave behind?

_____
_____
_____
_____
_____
_____
_____
_____
_____
_____
_____
_____

Name two or three people and your honest assessment of how they will react to your authenticity.

Chapter 7:
Nurturing Authentic Relationships

Real relationships are built on trust, respect, and sharing your true self without pressure or judgment. They're like cozy blankets for folks healing from fawn trauma because you can be you, and that's enough. You express yourself, feel understood, and fit right in. Forming authentic relationships is a big part of healing and growing.

Laying the Groundwork

Starting strong means having the following in your relationships:

- **Trust** is the glue that holds relationships together. You believe in others, and they believe in you. You build trust by being reliable and open, by setting clear boundaries, and by respecting other people's boundaries.

- **Mutual Respect** is all about accepting the differences in how you approach situations, welcome new people into your life, opinions about world events, even favorite cuisine. There is room for disagreement but not for disparaging each other's space and values. You're kind and understanding, and you expect the same in return.

- **Safe Place:** Relationships with trust at the center of them feel like home where you can be yourself. You speak honestly without being judged and return the same. You show you care by sharing your true feelings when others share their true feelings.

Creating a Solid Structure

Open and honest communication is the key to real relationships, but fawn trauma prevents us from trusting others and ourselves. Because our healing journeys are constant, we have to begin early putting these skills to work and use them consistently:

- **Really Listen:** When you chat, be all there. Listen for understanding and not to respond. You need to ascertain what the other person means, even if you don't agree. Listen without judging and let them know you hear them.

- **Peaceful Talk:** Communicate without hurting. Use "I" statements to express your feelings and needs. This way, you can say how you feel without blaming or criticizing the other party.

- **Stay Strong:** Exude confidence when you speak by being direct. You need to say what you mean and mean what you say. Keep their feelings in mind, but don't forget yours matter, too.

Fixing Things Up

If things get rough, here's how to smooth things out:

- **Face Conflict:** Handle problems with respect by admitting when you fall short. Talk about the situation calmly, really listen, and look for solutions that work for both people. If you need time to think about something or the other person needs some space, mutual respect means tabling the issue until you both come back to the table ready to talk.

- **Bye-Bye Toxicity:** If a relationship isn't good for you, it's okay to move on. Letting go is a way of saying you deserve better. Put your well-being first.

A Journey Worth Taking

Building authentic relationships is like growing a garden — it takes time and effort. Remain understanding, talk openly, and appreciate what makes each person special. Remember, being yourself helps others be themselves, too. Keep in mind, real relationships are like treasures — they heal, grow, and make life shine brighter.

Reflections

Your support network may include friends, family, support groups, and/or online communities.

What's important is that you surround yourself with people who validate your experiences, respect your boundaries, and support your healing journey.

> First, who are the individuals in your support network and why do you list them?

_____
_____
_____
_____
_____
_____
_____
_____
_____
_____
_____
_____
_____
_____
_____
_____

Now list any support groups or online communities you turn to for empathy and understanding.

Think about how you show up for other people in your life. Make a list of how you support and nurture your friends, family members, even colleagues.

_____
_____
_____
_____
_____
_____
_____
_____
_____
_____
_____
_____
_____
_____
_____
_____
_____
_____

_____
_____
_____
_____
_____
_____
_____
_____
_____
_____
_____
_____
_____
_____
_____
_____
_____

Now, write about how these same people show up for you.

_____
_____
_____

_____
_____
_____
_____
_____
_____
_____
_____
_____
_____
_____
_____
_____
_____
_____
_____

Compare the lists and highlight the points where you require more synergy for truly authentic relationships.

_____
_____
_____
_____

Chapter 8:
Self-Care for Authentic Living

Self-care isn't a luxury; think of it more like recharging your batteries so you can live authentically. You pamper your mind, body, and heart.

Self-care can be defined as a care package you send to yourself. It means recognizing what you need and making sure you get it. When you take time for rest, relaxation, and doing things that make you happy, you create a world where you come first so you're better equipped to be your true self in all that you do.

Daily self-care also encompasses a range of actions and practices that are focused on maintaining your physical, mental, and emotional well-being. It is the act of taking intentional steps to ensure that you are functioning at your best and able to meet life's demands effectively.

Setting and maintaining personal boundaries is a vital form of self-care. It involves clearly defining what is acceptable and what isn't in your interactions with others to prevent burnout, reduce stress, and preserve your mental and emotional energy. It also involves saying "no" when necessary to protect your time and well-being.

Financial self-care involves managing your finances correctly: budgeting, saving, investing, and paying bills on time. When you have control over your financial situation, you reduce stress and gain peace of mind, contributing to your overall well-being.

Maintaining a tidy and organized living space is another form of self-care. A clean home can have a positive impact on your mental state, reducing feelings of chaos and feeling overwhelmed. It creates an environment that promotes relaxation and focus, contributing to your overall sense of well-being.

Be proactive in protecting your physical, mental, and emotional health as you navigate the various aspects of your life. Set boundaries, manage finances, and keep your living space organized. This allows you to create a foundation of stability and wellness. You begin to thrive in your daily activities and maintain a healthy work-life balance. Self-care helps you recognize your needs and to take the necessary actions to meet them, ultimately fostering a more fulfilling and sustainable lifestyle.

Knowing What You Need

To design a self-care regimen, you need to know what makes you feel your best. Here's how to figure that out:

- **Physical Love:** Give your body what it needs; healthy food, movement, good sleep, and keeping your doctor and dentist appointments.

- **Emotional Bliss:** Focus on your feelings and what makes you happy and brings you peace. Think about what makes your heart smile; spending time with friends, writing in your journal, dancing, taking long walks, or talking to someone who cares.

- **Mental Clarity:** Give your mind a boost. Learn something new, get creative, or just do things that get your brain gears turning.

- **Social Time:** Hang with folks who make you feel like you. Spending time with supportive friends can do wonders to lift your spirits.

- **Soulful Moments:** What lights up your soul? Spiritual practice, spending time in nature, or simply some quiet reflection can all feel uplifting when you need it most.

Customizing Your Self-Care Plan

Once you know what floats your boat, create a plan that fits your groove using the following steps:

- **Put It on Your Schedule:** Treat self-care as you would any other important meeting.

Remember it's a must-do, not a maybe. Put it on your schedule and stick to it.

- **Plan It Out:** Decide what to do and when to do it. That could mean a daily dose or a weekly treat, depending on the activity.

- **Mix It Up:** You should have a variety of activities as part of your regimen, depending on what part of your health you're addressing. One morning you may walk for your physical health. You might meet a friend for coffee on a different day. Maybe you're sleeping in or scheduling a biweekly pedicure.

- **Stay in the Moment:** When you do your self-care activities, really be there. Savor the experience and let it recharge you.

Breaking Down Barriers

Sometimes life interrupts our self-care schedule or we make excuses about why we can't do this or that. Here's how to tackle those roadblocks:

- **Kick Guilt to the Curb:** You're not being selfish – you're being smart. Prioritize yourself without feeling guilty.

- **Set Boundaries:** Guard your self-care time like treasure. Let others know when you're taking a break and make it clear that it's important.

- **Simplify Life:** Make space for self-care by removing anything from your calendar that doesn't serve you. Prioritize what makes you feel awesome.

- **Ask for Help:** If it's tough, ask pals or pros for support. They can offer ideas, encouragement, and a little push when you need it.

Weaving Self-Care into Life

Self-care isn't a one-time thing; it's a lifestyle. Make it part of every day, like a good habit you can't live without. Little moments of self-care can add up to big changes over time.

And just like boundaries, what works for you today may not be what you need as your healing progresses. You are always captain of your journey. Stay kind to yourself and make self-care a lifelong love story.

Here are some additional examples of self-care activities:

1. Physical Self-Care:

Engage in regular physical activity to maintain fitness and reduce stress. Eat a balanced diet that nourishes your body and provides essential nutrients. Ensure you get enough quality sleep to rejuvenate your body and mind. Stay adequately hydrated by drinking enough water throughout the day. Schedule and attend medical and dental appointments for preventive healthcare.

2. Mental and Emotional Self-Care:

Practice mindfulness and meditation to reduce stress and promote mental clarity. Write down your thoughts and feelings to gain insight and emotional release. Seek professional help to address mental health concerns. Engaging in creative activities such as art, music, or writing for self-expression. Set boundaries on screen time to protect mental and emotional well-being.

3. Social and Relational Self-Care:

Spend time with friends and family who uplift and support you. Establish healthy boundaries in your relationships to protect your well-being. Address conflicts constructively to maintain healthy relationships. Carve out solitude when needed to recharge and reflect.

4. Spiritual Self-Care:

Take time to connect with your spiritual beliefs for inner peace and guidance. Spend time in nature to find spiritual renewal. Engage in acts of service or volunteering to promote a sense of purpose.

5. Time Management and Productivity Self-Care:

Practice setting clear priorities and focusing on what matters most to you. Declining commitments that overwhelm you and learn to say "no" when necessary. Make time for your favorite hobbies and interests to bring you joy and relaxation.

6. Sensory Self-Care:

Using scents like essential oils to create a calming or invigorating atmosphere. Enjoying a warm bath or shower to relax and rejuvenate your mind and body. Listening to soothing music to elevate your mood.

It's critical to explore and discover self-care activities that resonate with you and incorporate them into your routine to promote overall well-being.

Reflections

Prioritize self-care activities that bring you joy, relaxation, and a sense of well-being. This could include hobbies, spending time in nature, taking baths, practicing self-care rituals, or engaging in creative outlets.

What are at least three self-care activities have you chosen?

_____
_____
_____
_____
_____
_____
_____
_____

When will you schedule them?

_____
_____
_____
_____

Learning healthy coping mechanisms to regulate your emotions and manage stress is a form of self-care. This could include deep breathing exercises, meditation, journaling, physical activity, or seeking support from loved ones and friends.

What coping mechanisms have you chosen to manage your emotions and stress?

_____
_____
_____
_____
_____
_____
_____
_____
_____
_____
_____
_____
_____
_____
_____
_____
_____
_____

Are they working for you, or do you need to choose new options?

Chapter 9:
Building Resilience on the Path to Authenticity

Authenticity is not a destination but an ongoing process. Your commitment to showing up as your true self in every moment, embracing your strength and vulnerability, and continually growing and evolving is all about resilience; your ability to hold firm when old thought patterns and behaviors threaten to disrupt the progress you made.

The previous chapters guided us through understanding the roots of fawn trauma, recognizing its impact on our lives, and providing practical strategies to heal, discover, and reclaim our true selves. Each step, from understanding childhood experiences to practicing self-compassion to setting boundaries and practicing self-care has contributed to the holistic process of becoming more authentic.

By integrating these principles into our lives, we empower ourselves to break free from the cycle of people-pleasing, self-betrayal, and disconnection. We embraced our vulnerability, removed our masks, and integrated self-compassion to navigate challenges, build meaningful relationships, and live a life aligned with our true values and desires.

Recovering from fawn trauma response requires an on-going commitment to personal growth. Every action you take to reinforce your boundaries adds to your resilience. Every positive comment you make to yourself to contradict your inner critic builds your resilience.

Honestly, sometimes it's exhausting and you will want to give up and just return to your "normal" life. And I know you know this, but those days are over because you deserve to live a real life that is of your own making and not what you were told your life should be.

You understand the roots of your fawning behavior, and now is your time to heal and develop healthier patterns of relating to yourself and others. Remember, this is a journey, and progress will almost certainly be nonlinear. Still, every step forward strengthens your resilience.

Celebrate every step forward and be gentle with yourself along the way. You deserve a fulfilling life on your terms, and soon you won't even remember what your life was like before you developed your deep core of resilience.

As we move forward, remember that our journeys are as unique as we are. Take what resonates, adapt it to your circumstances, and continue learning and growing. Celebrate your progress and acknowledge that growth takes time. Be patient with yourself and practice self-love as you move forward.

You have the power to create a life that reflects your true self free of the fawn trauma that marked too much of your life. Embrace your unique qualities, honor your needs, and show up as the real you. Keep nurturing your self-awareness, practice self-care, and cultivate authentic connections. By doing so, you add to your resiliency to weather the tough stuff that comes with living a human life. Continue to flourish and inspire others with your journey of healing, growth, and authentic living.

Embracing authenticity is indeed a lifelong journey, and your understanding of its essence shines through everything you do. May your path be filled with growth, self-discovery, and the deep fulfillment that comes from living in alignment with your true self. May you continue finding strength, connecting with others who resonate with your genuine self, and inspiring positive change in the world.

The path toward your true self, your authenticity, is an ongoing adventure, and as you take steps forward, I send you joy, fulfillment, and a deep sense of purpose. Remember that you have the strength within you to lead a life that's authentically yours, and your efforts create ripples for those around you. Here's to a life filled with all you need to be exactly who you are.

Final Reflection

What is your overall plan in addressing and responding to your trauma? How are you nurturing your mind, body, and spirit; therapy, meditation, yoga, etc.?

_____
_____
_____
_____
_____
_____
_____
_____
_____
_____
_____
_____
_____
_____
_____
_____

When do/did you start?

_____
_____
_____
_____

Have you seen evidence of your desired outcome? In what way?

_____
_____
_____
_____
_____
_____
_____
_____
_____
_____
_____
_____
_____
_____

YOU are a Fawn Trauma Crusher!

I want you to know that you are a true warrior on a journey of healing, strength, and self-discovery. The path you are on may be challenging but remember that the process of healing from fawn trauma is a testament to your incredible resilience and courage.

By picking up this book and taking part in the journaling exercises, you took your first steps towards reclaiming your power and finding your authentic self. The journey to healing is not a straight line, and there may be moments when you feel overwhelmed or doubt your progress. In those moments, please remember that healing is about progress, not perfection.

You are rewriting your story, one step at a time. Just like a flower that pushes through the cracks in the pavement to bloom, you are emerging stronger and more beautiful than before. Your journey is uniquely yours, and every victory, no matter how small, is a step toward reclaiming your agency and finding your voice.

Surround yourself with love and support – from friends, family, or professionals who understand and uplift you. You don't have to do this alone. And never forget to extend the same kindness and patience to yourself that you would offer to a dear friend.

The journey ahead might be filled with ups and downs, but each day you wake up and face it head-on, you're winning the battle against the shadows of the past. Your worth is immeasurable, and your capacity for healing knows no bounds.

Believe in yourself, for you have already demonstrated incredible strength by embarking on this journey. The scars you carry are a testament to your survival, and they will eventually become symbols of triumph and growth.

Keep moving forward, keep embracing your true self, and keep believing in the power of your voice. You deserve all the love, happiness, and peace that life has to offer.

With unwavering support and admiration,

Tracey

Appendix: Resources for Further Exploration

During your healing journey, you may find valuable the additional resources listed here. This appendix provides a list of recommended books, websites, and organizations that can offer further support and guidance.

Books:

1. "The Body Keeps the Score: Brain, Mind, and Body in the Healing of Trauma" by Bessel van der Kolk

2. "Complex PTSD: From Surviving to Thriving" by Pete Walker

3. "The Gifts of Imperfection: Let Go of Who You Think You're Supposed to Be and Embrace Who You Are" by Brené Brown

4. "The Authenticity Principle: Resist Conformity, Embrace Differences, and Transform How You Live, Work, and Lead" by Ritu Bhasin

5. "Self-Compassion: The Proven Power of Being Kind to Yourself" by Kristin Neff

Websites and Online Resources:

1. National Alliance on Mental Illness (NAMI) - www.nami.org

2. Psychology Today - www.psychologytoday.com

3. The Authenticity Institute - www.authenticityinstitute.com

4. The Greater Good Science Center - www.greatergood.berkeley.edu

5. Inner Integration - www.innerintegration.com (specializes in healing from narcissistic abuse)

Organizations and Support Groups:

1. Adult Survivors of Child Abuse (ASCA) - www.ascasupport.org

2. Survivors of Incest Anonymous (SIA) - www.siawso.org

3. National Sexual Assault Hotline - 1-800-656-4673 (RAINN)

4. Adult Children of Alcoholics (ACA) - www.adultchildren.org

5. Mental Health America - www.mhanational.org

Please note this is not an exhaustive list, and there are many other valuable resources available. It is important to find the ones that resonate with you personally and align with your specific needs and circumstances.

Remember to approach your healing journey at your own pace, seeking support when needed and honoring your unique process. You are not alone, and there are resources and communities available to assist you every step of the way.

May these resources provide you with additional tools, insights, and connections to further support your path toward healing, authenticity, and a life filled with purpose and joy.

Disclaimer: The resources listed here are for informational purposes only and should not replace professional advice or therapy. It is recommended to consult with qualified professionals or therapists for personalized guidance.

Our deepest fear is not that we are inadequate.

Our deepest fear is that we are powerful beyond measure.

It is our light, not our darkness that most frightens us.

We ask ourselves, who am I to be brilliant, gorgeous, talented, fabulous?

Actually, who are you not to be?

You are a child of God.

Your playing small does not serve the world.

There is nothing enlightened about shrinking so that other people won't feel insecure around you.

We are all meant to shine, as children do.

We were born to make manifest the glory of God that is within us.

It is not just in some of us; it is in everyone.

And as we let our own light shine, we unconsciously give other people permission to do the same.

As we are liberated from our own fear, our presence automatically liberates others."

Marianne Williamson, from A Return To Love: Reflections on the Principles of A Course in Miracles (Harper Collins, 1992; Chapter 7, Section 3)

www.ingramcontent.com/pod-product-compliance
Lightning Source LLC
Chambersburg PA
CBHW051618010526
44119CB00008B/194